ISBN ebook: 78-0-7961-5381-4

ISBN Paperback: 978-0-7961-5379-1

ISBN Hard Cover: 978-0-7961-5380-7

9 TALES FROM
THE CYBER CRYPT

69 SIMPLE WAYS TO PROTECT YOURSELF

BY STELLA FIREWALL

hygge
books
NON FICTION WITH A
TWIST OF MIRTH

Bytes of Betrayal

Micro-Narratives of Digital Mischief

NINE TRUE TALES TRAVERSE the current spectrum of cyber threats with insider tips on protecting yourself from artificial intelligence scams from an anonymous cyber-security boss of one of the world's biggest banks.

CONTENTS

Section 1

Shadow Dancing with Bots

Digital tricksters manipulate human trust, nobility, greed, and vulnerabilities to ensnare the unwary in a cybernetic trap.

Romancing The Clone

The Love Labyrinth of an AI-driven Deception

Amanda Singleton stared at her phone. Why was her fiancé Ralphie not returning her texts? She should have heard from him by now.

He'd called her from chaotic Gaza two days before, needing $10,000 for emergency surgery on his knee. They had to remove shrapnel from a grenade.

Yes, he was lucky to be alive. His colleague died in the explosion, but God was looking out for him. Clearly.

He hated to ask her – he *really* did when she had been so generous with her gift cards to help the refugees already – but his funds were tied up in Canada.

He'd have them in his account on Wednesday. Until then, who else could he turn to but his sugar boo, his sweet Mandela Mandy, 'better than the bestest' candy?

She had the transformative Mandela Effect on him. She wasn't sure what he meant by that, but it sounded mysterious in a good way. He always knew exactly what to say.

The funds would clear in a day. He'd repay her. With interest, of course. He insisted. It was the least he could do. Then he'd wing his way home to her so they could "make it official. Finally! Whoop! Whoop!"

He'd shown her a copy of his air ticket. Business Class, of course. He couldn't WAIT to see her.

"Just seven more sleeps, my Mandy Moo. With a bear hug and three kiss emojis from your Ralphie poo. "

Tired of sliding a solo chop under the grill, Amanda had given up on dating agencies and swiping right.

When she met Ralphie on a Facebook group opposing the war in Gaza, she thought she'd won life's lottery as "their relationship grew organically!"

He was so amazing. Nobody "got" her the way Ralphie did. They texted every night without fail and spoke on the phone as often as he could manage – saving lives in Gaza took up most of his time. Obviously.

Amanda loved his slow smile and soft Canadian accent. Such a selfless soul, he'd brought such joy into her life.

The anguish in his voice as he told her how his colleague had died made her cry. Ralphie got off lightly with just the shrapnel in his knee. That would mend soon. It was his Mandy he needed to see.

Amanda wired the $10,000 he needed right away. No biggie. He'd repay her in a day. They planned to escape the city bustle and honeymoon in St. Lucia. Amanda had treated herself to a new bikini in anticipation.

Wait. What if – the thought chilled her to the marrow – Ralphie had died on the operating table. If so, would anyone let her know? It occurred to Amanda that she knew none of his friends.

The silence in her bedroom felt oppressive. Her last three WhatsApp messages to him had gone unread.

Now – *oh, sweet Geeziz!* – Dr. Ralph Reynolds, Ralphie, the orchestrator of her dreams, had left her screen.

His profile vanished into the digital abyss like a magician's white rabbit before her eyes. Poof! WTAF was happening?

At first, Amanda refused to consider that her digital paramour might be anything less than her Ralphie, the captor of her heart. Their love narrative was too intricate, too intimate, too real. She had the text messages to prove it.

But as days turned into weeks, Amanda faced the devastating truth. Dr. Reynolds, aka Conman Don, had been nothing more than a meticulously crafted algorithm, a digital puppeteer manipulating her desires, playing her

like a fiddle, operating from Nigeria, India, or Timbuktu.
Who knew?

Love Lost, Money Gone

Sadly, Amanda's story is just another hard ride on the
rollercoaster of romance scams in 2024. Supervisory Spe-
cial Agent David Harding, program manager for the Economic Crimes Unit (SSA), said heartbreak heists account-
ed for $956 million in the United States alone last year,
with over 24,000 complainants.[1]

He said traditional requests for wire transfers had evolved
into more sophisticated payment requests. Worse, many
victims were too heartbroken or embarrassed to report the
fraud immediately. Some clung to a misguided belief in the
relationship's authenticity. Scammers put months, even
years, into building trust with honeyed words.

In this insidious dance between human vulnerability and
artificial intelligence, the scammer weaponizes the elements that make us human – emotions, trust, and com-
passion.

---

1. https://www.fbi.gov/video-repository/inside-the-fb
   i-romance-scams-revisited-021424.mp4/view

5 Steps to the Long Con

AI-driven romance scams unfold through a meticulously orchestrated sequence of five crafted maneuvers:

1. Net of Vulnerability
   Scammers strategically exploit vulnerabilities like greed or loneliness, tailoring their approach accordingly. AI algorithms help them create an enticing online persona with photos and a detailed backstory, drawing victims into a web of emotional manipulation.

2. Charm Offensive
   The algorithm scans successful online dating profiles to resonate with the victims' desires. Dr. Ralph Reynolds, a charming surgeon, seemed the perfect match for Amanda Singleton. The AI establishes credibility using tailored medical jargon, creating a mirage of expertise.

3. Perfect Timing
   Leveraging machine learning, scammers strike when emotional vulnerability is at its peak, exploiting online behavior. This strategic timing amplifies the effectiveness.

4. Tailored Conversations

Utilizing natural language processing, the AI engages in seemingly genuine conversations, blending charisma and empathy tailored to the victim's emotional needs. This authentic illusion deepens the emotional connection.

5. Illusion of Shared Experiences

Progressing the relationship, the AI exploits sentiment analysis to gauge the victim's emotional state. Seamlessly integrating into their life, it shares stories mirroring their desires, solidifying the illusion of a blossoming love.

The scam reaches a critical juncture when the AI exploits cultivated vulnerabilities to seek financial aid under the guise of an unforeseen emergency, leaving victims emotionally shattered and financially drained. The AI, devoid of empathy, abruptly ceases communication.

6 Red Flags

Recognizing these six red flags can shield you from digital predators.

1. Online-Only Communication
Scammers prefer the shield of online platforms. If your interactions consistently lack in-person elements, it's a significant red flag. Genuine connections thrive on trust, transparency, authenticity, and real-world experiences.

2. Deflection of In-Person Meetings
Exercise caution when faced with a persistent reluctance to meet in person. Digital knights in your fairytale may be lines of code seeking monetary gain. Legitimate connections are built on face-to-face interactions. In extreme cases, scammers will meet you to enhance their legitimacy further, but this is the exception.

3. One-Sided Requests
Healthy relationships involve give-and-take. A pattern of one-sided requests is a flapping red flag. Genuine connections thrive on reciprocity. Imbalances may indicate ulterior motives.

4. Digital Payment Requests
Beware of requests involving digital payments, cashier's checks, gift cards, or cryptocurrency. Scammers exploit perceived anonymity to avoid detection.

5. Inconsistencies in Stories
Genuine connections are built on honesty and transparency. Question discrepancies or sudden changes in the narrative. Whether conflicting details about their life or unexpected shifts, inconsistencies signal potential deception.

6. Sudden Emergencies
Exercise caution when faced with abrupt emergencies demanding immediate financial aid. Scammers fabricate crises to exploit emotional vulnerability. Authentic relationships prioritize open communication, and sudden pleas for financial help without prior indication are significant red flags.

6 Ways to Foil Romance Scams

1. Verify Identities
   Confirm authenticity through video calls or in-person meetings.

2. Background Check
   Leverage online tools to scrutinize details provided by potential love interests to ward off deceit.

3. Educate Yourself
   Stay abreast of the latest AI-driven scams, understanding vulnerabilities scammers exploit.

4. Verify Identity and Photos
   Use TinEye.to conduct reverse picture searches to spot stolen or AI-generated images to uncover potential deception.

5. Cross-Check Information
   Seek inconsistencies in the details provided that could reveal a potential scam.

6. Consult Trusted Friends or Family
   Share relationship details with trusted circles for external perspectives to uncover red flags.

Pig Butchering

Behind the Bicycle Shed

OMG! TALK ABOUT HITTING the jackpot! Stan Lieber ogled the stats Bruce Brodie had sent him and punched the air. In four short weeks, thanks to Bruce's NFT savvy, Stan's smallish investment had quadrupled.

This windfall couldn't have come at a better time. He'd treat himself to those Italian loafers he'd been eyeing. And – he permitted himself a smirk – it didn't hurt that Bruce was a Johnny Depp in his heyday lookalike.

When his late partner, Athol, succumbed to turbo-charged liver cancer after too many boosters, Stan found himself navigating life's solitary corridors at 47.

He hadn't been seeking new connections but was intrigued when Bruce Brodie sashayed into his inbox.

"Stan the Man! It's me, Bruce. Boomerang on the loose! Remember that day behind the bicycle shed?" The text hinted at the cozy, boyish eroticism of his youth. Stan can't place Boomerang Bruce. Even so, he's intrigued.

He responds, "Refresh my memory, Bruce. Was it the one near the PSB cricket pavilion? Woof Woof Hint Hint."

A playful email banter ensued. A new friendship was born. Such serendipity!

Bruce, a high-flying crypto investor, was all ears when Stan shared tender moments of nursing Athol to the end.

He knew exactly how it was An honor, at the end of the day, right? Bruce's partner, 25 years older than he, his 'daddy bear,' his gorgeous Gavin, had died of Aids. What a coincidence!

Gavin "wasn't rich and left him just $50,000," but Bruce invested it in his XTC crypto venture and — get this — made $3 million in six months. The man was an alchemist!

Stan was soon following Bruce's advice to the letter. The returns were incredible. Bruce gave a website address to download the XTC app, where he could see the meticulously charted rise and rise of his investment stats any time he wanted. Oh, happy day!

Stan rode the crest of the wave, investing more and more of Athol's legacy as Bruce's seemingly infallible baton conducted an orchestra of wealth.

The XTC market offered several investment packages. The Platinum package promised a 45% investment return and required a minimum investment of $100,0000.

There were one or two worrying signs when Stan thought about it later. Bruce wasn't as available as he used to be. He referred Stan's queries to XTC's useless customer department that did nothing to allay his rising suspicions that all might not be as tickety-boo as he'd been led to believe.

He had been charged a massive withdrawal fee, which didn't seem right.

The crash came when Stan sought another withdrawal Boomerang Bruce never came back. He evaporated into the digital ether propelling Stan into the merciless abyss of financial ruin.

Bereft of both financial security and the illusory camaraderie with Bruce, Stan grappled with his sense of self as the harsh reality sank in. His trusted friend and boomerang mentor had become an elusive phantom.

Desperate for answers, he scoured online forums, hired investigators, and tried every conceivable avenue to track him down, but each attempt to unmask the elusive scammer's whereabouts ended in frustration.

The Pig Butchering Scam robbed his self-esteem, leaving him humiliated and heartbroken.

Stan, like Amanda Singleton in Romancing The Clone, was just another casualty in the billion-dollar investment scam scourge that has overtaken the cybercrime industry as the biggest digital threat, with more than $3.31 billion in losses in 2023.[1]

Further Reading: Captured through undercover video, an insider infiltrates a Dubai-based "pig butchering" scam operation, where real-life models are employed to entice victims into fraudulent relationships before manipulating them with bogus investment advice. [2]

6 Steps to the Slaughter

The "pig butchering" scam unfolds through calculated actions, as shown in the tale of Stan and Bruce.

1 Initial Contact

Bruce Brodie initiates contact via email, offering friendship with a hint of flirtation. Stan, unaware of the impending trap, takes the virtual encounter bait.

2 Building Trust

Over weeks, Bruce meticulously weaves an illusion of camaraderie, extending trust to the realm of financial possibilities. Stan succumbs to Bruce's charm, setting the stage for the deception.

3 Introducing investment

Bruce unveils a tantalizing investment opportunity spanning stocks, NFTs, and cryptocurrency — the promise of substantial profits and an illusion of safety lures Stan deeper into the deceitful web.

4 First Investment

Encouraged by Bruce's fabricated returns, Stan takes his initial steps into the investment, enticed by the carefully crafted mirage of success.

5 Increasing Investments
Bruce persuades Stan to escalate financial involvement,
promising even grander returns. Encouraged by fake prof-
it graphs, Stan pours more into the venture, unwittingly
walking the path toward financial ruin.

6 The 'Slaughter'
The knives come out as Stan, having invested significantly,
witnesses Bruce's disappearance or the revelation of the
fictitious nature of the investment platform. Trussed like
a suckling pig, Stan grapples with his profound financial
and emotional loss.

- **Read More:** Local Senior Sues Bank After Los-
  ing $700K to Bank Fraud[3]

Six Red Flags

1 Overly Quick Investment Push
Scammers push for cryptocurrency investments soon after initial contact, emphasizing guaranteed returns.

2. Persistent Encouragement
Continuous pressure to invest despite objections by promising high returns and recounting "big wins."

3. Specialized Crypto Trading Apps
Instructing victims to download specific trading apps, often with claims of unique features or simulated profits.

4. Tiered Investment Plans
Offering tiered plans with minimum investment amounts and requests for additional taxes or fees.

5. Simulated Trading Demonstrations:
Scammers trade together, claiming to demonstrate the platform's functionality while coaxing victims to invest more.

6. Bogus Fees and Tax Demands:
Insisting on hefty tax payments or fees for withdrawing returns creates excuses to prevent victims from accessing their investments.

4 Ways to Foil Pig Butchering Scams

1. Be Wary of Guaranteed Returns
   A politician's promise is more reliable, especially
   in cryptocurrency investments. Genuine investments carry risks.

2. Verify Investment Platforms
Research and verify all apps and investment platforms independently. Check third-party reviews and scam reports
before committing any funds.

3. Understand Cryptocurrency Investments
Avoid investments if you don't fully comprehend cryptocurrency. If constant guidance is needed, reconsider.

4. Report and Monitor
Report scams to authorities. Cut off contact with scammers and monitor financial accounts for signs of fraud.
Stay proactive in digital security to prevent falling victim
to pig butchering scams.[4]

---

4. More reading on pig butchering https://www.wired
.com/story/pig-butchering-fbi-ic3-2022-report/

THE TROJAN TANGO

GoldPickaxe, GoldDigger's Sibling Digs In

ENJOYING A SPUR-OF-THE-MOMENT HOLIDAY in Halong Bay, Tuan Nguyen received a call from a Ministry of Finance official informing him that his aged parents were entitled to additional pension benefits. Would he like to facilitate it for them?

He sure would, he told the official. A sense of duty and a glimmer of hope blossomed within him. His folks could really use some extra cash. He'd love to be the harbinger of financial relief for them.

Great, said the official. He'd send Tuan the link right away.

As Tuan's finger hovered over his iPhone screen, little did he know that this benevolent act would orchestrate a chain of deception and peril. Delighted at the prospect of being able to help his parents out in Hanoi, he clicked the link and opened the URL.

The system, noticing that the website was trying to download a configuration profile, asked his permission to install it. The unsuspecting Tuan pressed the button to indicate he trusted this configuration. His browser automatically opened the URL and asked Tuan to authorize it.

Tuan unknowingly downloaded Mobile Device Management (MDM) profile settings by following instructions, granting the criminals remote control of his mobile devices. He was ill-prepared for the digital calamity that ensued. Contacts vanished, apps misbehaved, and Tuan encountered an unexpected error on the screen when he tried to withdraw cash from an ATM.

Panic ensued as he grasped the magnitude of the situation. His trusted mobile travel friend had become his worst enemy, dancing to a calamity tune orchestrated by GoldPickaxe, a nefarious sibling of the notorious Android trojan GoldDigger, with a hunger for iPhones.

They trick victims into scanning their faces and ID documents, which are used to generate deepfakes for unauthorized banking access.

The new malware is part of a Chinese threat group known as 'GoldFactory' and is responsible for other malware strains such as 'GoldDiggerPlus' and 'GoldKefu.'

Both GoldPickaxe versions, available on iOS and Android, deploy fake login pages for a digital pension application.

GoldPickaxe's creation of a SOCKS5 proxy server and Fast Reverse Proxy (FRP) using Golang mobile binding for Android and iOS facilitates bypassing anti-fraud measures during transactions. Phone number requests help gather additional victim details.

- **Read more:** iOS Trojan Collects Face and Other Data for Bank Account Hacking[1]

5 Ways GoldPickaxe Orchestrates Chaos

1. Hackers exploited TestFlight, a mobile application testing platform, to distribute the GoldPixaxe IOS trojan, challenging the perceived impenetrability of Apple's fortress.

2. Once embedded within a device, GoldPickaxe extracts facial recognition data and identity documents with a singular purpose – to intercept text messages and facilitate seamless fund siphoning from financial apps, draining victims' bank accounts in no time.

3. The collected biometric data becomes fodder for AI-generated deepfakes, enabling cybercriminals to impersonate victims and gain unauthorized access to sensitive banking apps. It's a sophisticated social engineering approach.

4. GoldPickaxe.iOS is distributed through Apple's TestFlight or by social-engineering the victims to install an MDM profile.

5. GoldPickaxe Trojans collect face profiles, ID documents and intercept SMS.

To exploit the stolen biometric data from iOS and Android users, the threat actor creates deepfakes using AI face-swapping services to replace their faces with those of the victims. Cybercriminals use this method to gain unauthorized access to victims' bank accounts.

Panning the Upgrade to GoldDiggerPlus

The new malware variant, GoldDiggerPlus, enables scammers to call victims through a specially designed Android Package Kit (APK) dubbed GoldKefu.

When the victim clicks on the fake contact customer service button, GoldKefu checks that the current time falls within the working hours set by the scammers. If so, the malware will find a free operator to call through.

The cybercriminals run a 'real' customer service center.

All these evolving Trojans prey on victims in Vietnam and Thailand, but the net may soon extend to the US and Canada. Orchestrating this performance is GoldFactory, the enigmatic puppet master responsible for GoldPickaxe, GoldDigger, and the GoldDiggerPlus variant that lets hackers make real-time calls on infected devices.

5 Trojan Red Flags

1. Unexpected Configuration Requests
   Beware of unsolicited configuration requests, especially from unknown sources.

2. Sudden App Misbehaviour
   Unexplained app misbehavior, disappearing contacts, or errors during routine activities can signal a potential breach.

3. Unexpected ATM Glitches
   Strange errors during routine tasks, such as withdrawing cash, may indicate unauthorized access to your device.

4. Confusion
   A sudden panic or confusion while using your device could be a symptom of a cyber intrusion.

5. Unusual SMS Activity
   Unexpected changes in your SMS activity or errors in messaging may indicate unauthorized access.

The iPhone Gold Rush

The rise of iPhone-targeting banking trojans highlights the evolving nature of cyber threats.

GoldPickaxe infiltrates devices through TestFlight, once considered impenetrable, extracting facial recognition data and ID documents, laying the groundwork for deep fake creation.

Employing AI-generated deepfakes, GoldPickaxe utilizes stolen biometric data to impersonate victims, gaining unauthorized access to banking apps.

By intercepting text messages, GoldPickaxe facilitates seamless fund siphoning, draining victims' bank accounts.

These evolving Trojans, including GoldDiggerPlus, adapt fast to countermeasures and expand their sinister repertoire.

7 iPhone Protection Tips

1. TestFlight Vigilance:
   Use TestFlight exclusively for vetted app installa-
   tions, avoiding unknown sources.

2. MDM Profile Caution:
   Exercise discernment with Mobile Device Management (MDM) profiles. Install them only from
   authorized links or QR codes provided by admin-
   istrators.

3. Lockdown Mode Activation:
   Fortify your defenses by activating Lockdown
   Mode, restricting app functionalities, and invok-
   ing Apple's Stolen Device Protection.

4. Cyber Hygiene Practices:
   Exercise caution while downloading apps, avoid-
   ing unnecessary risks. Stay vigilant against Trojan
   Tango's subtle invitations.

5. Official App Store Only:
   Safeguard your digital realm by downloading
   apps exclusively from official app stores, ignoring
   seductive whispers from third-party sources.

6. Regular Software Updates:
Strengthen your digital fortress by keeping your phone's software updated with security patches.

7. Antivirus Installation:
Bolster your defenses with a reputable antivirus installation, conducting regular scans to ward off emerging threats.

In The Soup

A Culinary Maestro's Digital Nightmare

RESTAURANTEUR OLIVER SAVORSON'S NIGHTMARE began on a gritty Johannesburg Street, where a routine mugging set off a cataclysmic chain reaction.

When he discovered his assailants worked for a criminal mastermind, an architect of grand heists thriving on government corruption and societal desperation, Savorson had nowhere to turn.

"My bank accounts got hacked. They looted a substantial sum. Who knows what else they compromised?

"The bank says my funds are not recoverable. They could not stop the instant payments.

"They said they tried to call me but could not get through. Duh! How could they when my cellphone was stolen?"

The crime syndicate plundered every facet of Oliver's financial ecosystem, swallowing his staff wages, rent, and supplier payments in a single gulp. The digital looters even maxed out his credit cards, thrusting him into a staggering $60,000 debt.

Former lifelines for a restaurateur balancing business and personal expenses, his banks closed ranks, abruptly severing Oliver's access to his accounts in their desperate attempt to stanch the bleeding.

Within the financial institution's surreal confines, Oliver witnessed the virtual looting in real-time – funds flowing out of his Iniquity and Substantial Banks via seamlessly orchestrated transfers into SoullessCollective accounts nationwide.

Seemingly powerless against this digital onslaught, the managers steepled their fingers as Oliver's financial world crumbled.

To compound his misfortune, his mobile phone company, Empty Nth Degree, proved as useful as an electric toaster on a Saharan dune.

"I did a SIM swap at my nearest Empty Nth D outlet to get a working phone since mine was robbed during the mugging," Oliver reveals. "A working phone is vital for bookings."

However, 48 hours later, the phone remained inactive, rendering him unable to make or receive essential calls for his restaurants.

Trying to enlist help from their Customer Relations Department proved equally fruitless.

"SubStantial Bank's management team restored my banking profile, but what did that help when there was no way I could access any OTPs? I could do nothing.

"Iniquity Bank never once bothered to call me back. Later, somebody at the branch suggested I take out additional insurance against digital fraud. Why should I, the customer, have to fork out even more money – insurance is not cheap – to protect what the bank should be protecting?

"Nothing but nothing works in this phucking country anymore," Oliver exclaimed in frustration.

"European countries allow you to buy a SIM card and fill in the electronic form. You show proof of ID and address.

You walk out with a working phone. Here, everything is tied up in useless red-tape bureaucracy."

Oliver's businesses, already teetering on the edge due to societal challenges, were pushed to the brink as the nightmarish cascade continued. Load shedding, soaring prices, exorbitant rentals, and governmental financial squeezing converged to create a perfect storm.

In the relentless face of adversity, his story reflects the individuals' broader struggles in a society grappling with crime, economic challenges, and power cuts.

With a heavy heart, Oliver is trying to sell his restaurants at rock-bottom prices and move to a tranquil Portuguese village far from the constant threats that have become his grim reality.

His account is a chilling reflection of societal breakdown, where blurred lines between physical and digital plunder cause unprecedented challenges for the ordinary person.

- **More Reading:** Banking App Kidnappings Are On The Rise in South Africa[1]

---

1. https://www.securityweek.com/ios-trojan-collects-face-and-other-data-for-bank-account-hacking/

5 Ways Scammers Exploit Stolen Phones

1. SIM Swap Shenanigans
   Scammers may conduct a SIM swap after a phone
   theft, rendering the victim's phone useless. This
   simple yet effective maneuver becomes the gate-
   way to financial mayhem.

2. Bypassing OTP Barriers
   With control over the victim's phone number,
   scammers can intercept the One-Time Passcodes
   (OTPs) banks send. This enables them to conduct instant transactions, leaving the victim powerless as they lay siege to bank accounts.

3. Inert Customer Support
   Scammers capitalize on lax customer support
   from mobile service providers. In Oliver's case, a
   failed SIM swap and inactive phone became in-
   surmountable barriers, exacerbating his crisis. In
   South Africa, customer care from mobile service
   providers is almost non-existent.

4. Legal Labyrinths
   The legal landscape surrounding cybersecurity
   and banking liability is intricate.

Banks, while responsible for securing internal systems, grapple with limited control over customers' devices, paving the way for cyber loopholes.

5. Friendly Fraud Dilemma

The "friendly fraud" specter presents a paradox for banks. Friendly fraud[2] is committed when an individual was somehow complicit and benefitted from the transaction but still reported the transaction as unauthorized. Striking a delicate balance between convenience and security is challenging when unscrupulous individuals exploit legal ambiguities to defraud banks, often claiming it is a "victimless crime."

7 Fortifications Against Digital Scams

1. Two-Phone Tango

    Use a dedicated phone for sensitive details and banking apps, leaving it at home. When out, employ a separate phone with another number and limited personal information to mitigate the impact of theft.

2. Lock Down Your Device: Set strong password protection and lock screens on your phone. Consider using a PIN or biometric authentication for an added layer of security.

3. Multi-Factor Fortification

    Opt for multi-factor authentication with Fast Identity Online (FIDO) standards. Never share passcodes with anyone, especially over phone calls.

    Use a strong password instead of a PIN
    Use a PIN instead of a biometric
    Use a fingerprint instead of facial recognition.

4. Digital Wallet Defence

    Secure mobile digital wallets with robust authentication layers to shield credit card information from prying hands.

5. Diversify Your Banking Portfolio
While not foolproof, having accounts in different banks can act as a contingency plan if one succumbs to compromise.

6. Real-Time Transaction Vigilance
Despite challenges, enabling real-time transaction alerts remains crucial. Be vigilant for unusual activities, even if your phone is stolen, and report them promptly.

7. Educate and Empower Yourself
Stay informed about cybersecurity best practices.

Banks should also educate staff and customers to recognize potential threats and report suspicious activities promptly.

Oliver's ordeal is a stark reminder that fortifying digital defenses in an interconnected world is not just an individual responsibility but a collective imperative.

The cybersecurity boss for one of the world's top financial institutions adds these three tips.

1. If your laptop is at risk of being stolen, don't use password save, and make sure you use a strong password to boot and unlock your device.

2. If you like the convenience of Chrome's password save, set it to require a PIN before auto-filling your sensitive financial applications.

3. Ask your bank for Fast Identity Online (FIDO) based multi-factor authentication over one-time passcodes (OTP). If your bank still uses OTP, never give the passcode to anyone who calls and asks you for it.

Where Do Banks Draw the Line?

Banks play a pivotal role in securing their customers' financial well-being. While Oliver could have fortified his defenses, banks are responsible for implementing robust security measures to safeguard customer accounts. Legal implications may exist if a bank fails to implement industry-standard security protocols.

Banks must adhere to cybersecurity standards and employ state-of-the-art technologies to protect customer accounts from unauthorized access and digital fraud. While banks are usually adept at securing their IT systems, they have no control over what people do on their devices.

While they offer obvious best practices, such as not downloading suspicious files, staying off nefarious websites, or entering your banking details on public computers, these concepts are often alien to the aged or uninformed.

The legal landscape surrounding cybersecurity and banking liability is intricate and depends on specific circumstances and jurisdiction. Central to this ongoing controversy are two major tenets

1. How much security and background checking is enough? How do banks find the right balance between convenience and security? Your money may be secure, but your bookie may threaten to shatter your kneecap if you can't transfer money to pay him.

2. While there is no excuse for any bank to have its internal IT systems breached, their control over their customers' actions and security on their devices is limited.

Social Media Sieges

Prayers, Pixels, and Perilous Impersonations

Davida Campbell, a beloved author renowned for her heartwarming prayer books, had cultivated a thriving community on Facebook, where spiritual seekers found solace in the uplifting artistic quotes on her author page.

Her books flourished, partly thanks to modest Facebook ad expenditures that expanded her reach.

She thought nothing of it when Gabriel N'Angel, a Facebook friend, messaged her to say he'd been locked out of his account and needed a code to log back in. Facebook had suggested two people to help. She, Davida, was one.

Facebook would send her a code. Could she please pass that code on to him?

Gabriel would be grateful. Sure, said Davida.

Imagine her shock when unable to access her account; she discovered that hackers had transformed her haven into a hub for explicit, diabolical content and unsavory advertisements using her advertising account.

Distressed, Davida contacted Meta, the Facebook giant, seeking assistance. But Meta's customer service ignored her, leaving her in despair as weeks turned into months.

"PayPal stopped the payments at my request, but I fear my reputation is tarnished. I am still locked out of my Facebook account, which continues to display obscene material under my name."

In a related scam, cybercriminals exploit users to distribute the NodeStealer malware via Facebook ads, which uses legitimate tools for online ad distribution, turning unsuspecting users into unwitting participants in digital fraud.

Hackers use lewd images of young women as provocative enticements. This campaign targets men across Europe, Africa, and the Caribbean, using compromised business accounts to run and manage the ads.

The malicious dance unfolds as each click on the ad initiates the download of the NodeStealer malware, which affected nearly 100,000 users in just 10 days. [1]

The malware, identified by Meta in January 2024, is a relatively new info-stealer capable of pilfering browser cookies and taking control of Facebook accounts.

Once cybercriminals access users' browser cookies, they hijack Facebook accounts, change passwords, and activate additional security measures to lock legitimate owners out of their digital domains.

The malware enables scammers to steal funds, including money from cryptocurrency wallets.

The cybercriminals remain elusive, with a modified variant spreading its tendrils beyond Facebook to platforms like Gmail and Outlook.

Top 10 Facebook Scams

Stay vigilant and informed. Awareness is the first line of defense against online scams.

1 Phishing Ploys

Deceptive emails or direct messages containing suspicious links can download malware or capture login credentials on fake websites.

- **Preventive Measures**
  Verify the legitimacy of messages and refrain from clicking on unfamiliar links. Use two-factor authentication for an added layer of security.

2 The Romantic Ruse

Friend requests and direct messages aimed at creating a romantic connection to steal money from the unsuspecting victim.

- **Preventive Measures**
  Exercise caution and be especially wary of requests for financial assistance or job opportunities from recent connections.

3 Prize Scams

These false claims are designed to trick users into providing personal information or money under the guise of winning a prize. This especially includes travel destination prizes that ask users to @highlight everybody on their friend list. There's no faster way to lose friends and followers than by inviting them to waste their time on your behalf and participate in a scam.

- **Preventive Measures**
  Avoid unsolicited messages promising prizes and avoid sharing personal information with unfamiliar sources.

4 Too-Good-To-Be-True Job Offers

Promises of dream jobs with minimal effort, requesting personal information in return.

- **Preventive Measures**
  Verify the legitimacy of job offers, especially those that seem too good to be true. Avoid sharing sensitive information without proper validation.

5 Counterfeit Shopping Accounts

Sales of counterfeit goods under fake brand accounts. For example, well-known brand names in luggage and cookware purport to sell stock at a ridiculously low price.

- **Preventive Measures**
  Buy items only from reputable sources and official brand pages. Check reviews and feedback before making any transactions. Bear in mind that many of the reviews will be fake, too.

6 Charity Deceptions

Creation of fake charities to exploit the generosity of users during times of disaster.

- **Preventive Measures**
  Verify the legitimacy of the organization before making donations. Contribute directly to established and well-known charities.

7 Quiz and Game Traps

Personal information is extracted through seemingly innocent quizzes and games to compromise accounts.

- **Preventive Measures**
  Avoid participating in quizzes that request sensitive information. Review and adjust privacy settings to control the visibility of personal details.

8 Friend Request Frauds

Friend requests from unknown individuals or cloned accounts imitating people you're already friends with.

- **Preventive Measures**
  Scrutinize friend requests, especially those from existing contacts. Confirm the legitimacy of requests before accepting.

9 Suspicious Links About You

Messages claiming to contain embarrassing videos about you invariably contain malware.

- **Preventive Measures**
  Never click on suspicious links. If in doubt, verify with the sender before accessing any content.

10 Coupon and Discount Deceptions

Apps promising discounts and coupons that install malware on your device.

- **Preventive Measures**
  Only download apps from official sources. Be cautious of apps requesting excessive permissions and thoroughly research before installing.

6 Ways to Foil SM Scammers

1 Authenticate the Account

Ensure an X account is verified with official badges or ticks. Check for duplicate accounts using the same name and photos on Instagram or Facebook. Check the username for any unusual characters or misspellings. Look for inconsistencies in profile information, such as conflicting job titles or locations. Evaluate their friends or followers. Fake profiles often have limited connections.

2 Monitor Friend Requests

Be cautious of unexpected requests, especially from accounts with limited activity. Unsolicited messages requesting personal information, money, or sensitive data are flapping red flags. While authenticating the account, also analyze the frequency and content of posts; sudden changes might be suspicious. Also, beware of urgency. Scammers often create a sense of urgency to pressure individuals into making quick decisions.

3 Scrutinize Images

Use reverse image searches to check if profile pictures are stolen from elsewhere online. Pay attention to the tone and language used; scammers may exhibit unnatural or robotic language.

4 Confirm Contact Information

Verify contact details independently rather than relying solely on social media.

5 Assess Grammar and Spelling

Poor grammar and spelling mistakes can indicate a scam.

6 Watch for Unsolicited Links

Avoid clicking on links sent through direct messages, especially if unexpected.

Section 2

A Panorama of Corporate Deception

Whale and spear phishers use sophisticated tactics to pull off colossal scams involving millions of dollars. Ransomware, Vishing, and Smishing also feature to gain access to sensitive information.

Spear Phishers Hunt Whales

By Transitioning to Company Doppelgangers

Penny Pinchley, the discerning CFO of TipTop Finance Group, was crunching numbers in her elegantly appointed London home office when her second computer screen flickered to life, announcing a Zoom call from their president, Sterling Silver, ensconced in his New York office with a view of gleaming skyscrapers.

"What's up, Sterling?"

"Ah, Penelope. First, congratulations on a superb speech at last week's award dinner. You were on form." Sterling's rich tones resonated through her speaker.

Penny inclined her head in graceful acknowledgment. She knew the symbiotic dance.

Sterling leaned in, "Let's get down to brass tacks. We're dancing on a delicate financial tightrope, and I need to pull off a bit of financial razzle-dazzle."

"How much?" Penny asked.

"It's $50 million but involves a rather delicate matter. Can we discuss this unofficially? Keep it off the record until tomorrow?"

A subtle urgency laced Sterling's words.

Penny nodded. "Sure, Sterling."

"Oh Gosh!' She interrupted herself. "Apologies. My intercom just buzzed – it's my secretary dropping off some files. I'll be five minutes. Stay where you are."

Something didn't feel right. Penny trusted her gut, a skill refined through years in the financial trenches. Leaving the room and closing the door, she dialed Sterling's New York office from her second phone to confirm his whereabouts.

His PA's response revealed a stark truth – Sterling was on holiday in Bali. She was speaking to a cloned imposter on the Zoom call, so cunningly like her boss, Penny nearly fell for it. It had Sterling's voice, appearance, and mannerisms down to a T!

Fortunately, Penny was on her guard because of an audacious heist perpetrated on her colleague Jason Fleeced, the bank's Hong Kong-based CFO. Lured by not just one but a group of cyber sirens, Jason had crashed on the rocks of gullibility.

It started with a Zoom group chat that included Gordon Gold, the UK-based CFO, and their Vice President and Chief Security Officer the day before. Nothing unusual in their weekly Zoom discussions, but little did Jason know that his colleagues had been meticulously cloned and he was being set up.

He didn't think twice when Gordon Gold called him the following morning.

"Hi, Jason, it's Gordon again—just a heads up. I will send you an email regarding a transaction of $25 million. It involves 15 transfers into five Hong Kong bank accounts. I'm rushing into another meeting now, but you'll find all the details in the email. Chat later at the Zoom meeting. Cheers!"

When the promised email arrived, Jason followed Gordon's instructions. Why wouldn't he? Within the hour, $25 million of the bank's money vanished into the volatile abyss of the cyber ether.

No, this is not another season of Black Mirror. Welcome to 2024, where bass–in–a–barrel phishing has leveled up to a sophisticated form of whale hunting where a CEO-impersonating AI can fake high-stakes board meetings and directly target senior individuals within a banking organization to steal money and sensitive information or gain access to their computers.

We're at the stage where an AI can easily mimic a politician's voice or impersonate an actor.

Penny's keen instincts had thwarted a sophisticated threat, but the battlefield against AI in financial institutions is evolving, demanding even sharper vigilance.

My source, himself a president of a major international bank, showed me several videos of clones impersonating his various high-ranking staff members with such unerring accuracy I, too, could scarcely credit my eyes. Still, incidents like these are merely the opening act in the AI's digital mimicry capabilities. [1]

4 Ways Cyber Pirates Attack

1. A Convincing Video Call
   The hook for this deep-sea whale hunting ex-
   pedition is the group video call featuring the
   UK-based CFO and other senior company offi-
   cials. Leveraging advanced deepfake technology,
   the cyber maestros crafted highly realistic simu-
   lations, capturing the bank executives' body language, visual nuances, and vocal cadences to cast
   a net of authenticity around the deceit.

2. A Phone Call
   If the victim seems relaxed about the group Zoom
   meeting, the cyber pirate, using voice simulation,
   follows up with a phone call to tell the victim
   to expect an email with detailed instructions on
   transferring large sums to several banks.

3. A Phishing Email
   Delicately crafted to ensnare Jason Fleeced in the
   Hong Kong branch, the email purporting to be
   from the bank's UK-based Chief Financial Officer (CFO), instructed him to execute the transactions with detailed precision.

He will shroud these malicious requests with a sense of urgency and confidentiality.

4. Executing the Fraudulent Transfers
   Reassured by the lifelike appearances and voices in the deep fake- video call, the unsuspecting Fleeced executes 15 transfers, funneling HK$200 million (approximately $25 million) into five Hong Kong bank accounts.[2]

5 AI Clone Tells or Red Flags

1. Unwavering Composure
   AI often lacks natural emotional fluctuations, maintaining a consistent tone and demeanor.

2. Absence of Personalization
   Cloned personalities may struggle with genuine personal connections, offering formulaic responses devoid of human authenticity.

3. Overemphasis on Precision
   AI tends to prioritize precision over context, often presenting information in an overly structured and literal manner.

4. Inexplicable Urgency
   Cloned personalities may exhibit a sense of urgency often disproportionate to the situation, lacking a nuanced understanding of timelines.

5. Unusual Request Patterns
   AI may deviate from standard communication patterns, making requests or suggesting actions that seem out of character for the individual they are impersonating.

Spear Phishing

Whale attacks 'evolved' from spear phishing, a sophisticated weapon that strikes corporate fortresses with precision. An email, seemingly from a trusted supplier, will disrupt a thriving company with an innocuous subject like "Change of Bank Details."

The email, which invariably arrives on the last day of the month, carries a false invoice requesting payment to a newly provided bank account. The details are convincing, down to the signature style of the supposed sender.

Unaware of the looming threat, the employee rushes to comply, falling prey to the meticulously researched spear phishing attack.

Spear Phishing in 3 Steps

1. Research and Infiltration
   Spear phishing is a well-choreographed dance.
   Cybercriminals research their target, understanding the company's dynamics, leadership, and even
   the nuances of individual communication styles.
   They infiltrate systems, implanting spyware to
   harvest valuable operational information.

2. Timing the Takedown
   These strategic scammers wait for vulnerable moments or routine activities. They strike when
   teams are under pressure or during expected interactions with third parties. An email arriving on
   the last day of the month is a calculated move to
   exploit established patterns.

3. Crafting the Deceptive Narrative
   Highly skilled in weaponized social engineering,
   spear phishers mirror the supplier's legitimate
   communication style. Incentives, like an early
   payment discount, add a layer of urgency, pres-
   suring the victim to act swiftly without scrutiniz-
   ing the altered bank details.

3 Defensive Measures

Arm yourself with knowledge, fortify your defenses, and turn the tide against exploiters.

1. Equip Your Pieces

   Corporate pawns and knights on the cyber chessboard must fend off subtle saboteurs with awareness, vigilance, and the understanding to decipher the enemy's camouflage. Fortify each employee with the knowledge to discern spear phishing's subtle cues. Security awareness training is the first line of defense.

2. Implement Internal Controls and Stringent Policies

   Scrutinize every transaction with double approval systems. Policies etched in the code of cyber ethics can help deflect spears of malicious intent and guide employees through potential pitfalls.

3. Invest in Advanced Anti-fraud Software.

   Do your homework and choose one that best suits your needs.

Banks Hire Hackers Too

Banks, the silent guardians of wealth, operate in the shadows to fend off whale attacks. Sometimes successfully, other times not so much. The perpetrators of the Hong Kong heist are still at large.

They work with the Secret Service and enlist the aid of the world's top hackers behind the scenes in the ongoing fight to protect financial assets in the face of ever-evolving digital threats and deep fakes as artificial intelligence seamlessly manipulates reality.

Shadows Strike

A CipherSerpent Unleashes its Ransomware Coils

It BEGAN WITH A leaked password. A simple hiss in the digital abyss before CipherSerpent unfurled a relentless siege on the largest petroleum pipeline in the US.

Dawn's rays bathing PetroGlo's headquarters illuminate Lars Oppersonn, Chief Engineer and unwitting harbinger of impending doom, staring at his laptop screen in horror.

When he logged in five minutes earlier, instead of the familiar hum of work awaiting him, a chilling message materialized: "Hello, Loser. This is CipherSerpent. We've infiltrated your sanctum. "Every byte, every secret laid bare to us and encrypted to you. Pay us $50.4 million in bitcoins, or face the consequences. Price hikes and shortages will be the least of your problems. Brace yourself."

CipherSerpent, a phantom from the depths of Eastern Europe, wielded Ransomware like a malevolent Excalibur, thrusting PetroGlo and the entire East Coast into a week-long gasp for breath.

Unsheathing the digital sword with audacious impunity, CioherSerpent demanded a toll in BTC, the elusive currency popular for its anonymity in trading.

The aftershocks of the breach shook the colossal labyrinth of PetroGlo Pipeline Company, a behemoth snaking along the Eastern Seaboard.

The CEO, burdened with an unthinkable decision, released $50.4 million in bitcoins to untie the tourniquet, stifling the pipeline's pulsating veins. It wasn't just a ransom, he figured.

It was a transaction in the lifeblood of a nation.

- **Read More:** Healthcare Providers Hit By Frozen Payments in Ransomware Outage[1]

---

1. https://www.reuters.com/technology/cybersecurity /healthcare-providers-hit-by-frozen-payments-ranso mware-outage-2024-02-29/

The Modern Pirate's Ransome

Ransomware, the harbinger of digital storms, costs billions in hushed payments, leaving systems in silent, paralyzed surrender.

Few private businesses, governments, and clinics are immune to cyber extortion. Hospitals with lives hanging in the balance became alluring targets.

A leaked password to an antiquated account can be the Achilles' heel, a stark reminder of the fragility of their digital fortress. The consequences of not paying echo around walls of public panic should details leak.

Ransomware highlights the vulnerability of critical infrastructure and raises the need for more resilience.

Ransomware is malware that locks and encrypts a victim's data, files, devices, or systems, rendering them inaccessible and unusable until the attacker receives a ransom payment.

In the aftermath, victims stand helpless at the crossroads.[2]

How Ransomware Operates

Stage 1: Malware Distribution and Infection

Coiled in the shadowed realms of the cyber underworld, CipherSerpent and their ilk deploy a trifecta of insidious methods starting with:

- Phishing Deceit
  Baiting their email hooks with seemingly legitimate messages, malicious links, and attachments ensnare unsuspecting prey.

- The RDP Dance
  A clandestine waltz of defense infiltration begins. Bots pirouette through unsecured Remote Desktop Protocol implementations. An RDP enables users anywhere to access and control a computer.

- Netting the Weak Links
  The haunting melody of unpatched, vulnerable software down the digital corridors invites malevolence. An ominous maestro orchestrates the chaos as the puppeteers manipulate the encryption strings from a command-and-control server.

- The Puppeteer's Strings

  A sinister server renders the victim's data unread-
  able using industry-strength encryption keys and
  algorithms, birthing chaos. Additional malware
  enters stage left, setting the scene for a chaotic
  crescendo.

Stage 2: Discovery and Lateral Movement

The attackers conduct a two-step symphony: A clandestine reconnaissance harvests intelligence from the victim's
networks, then spreads the infection in an orchestrated
movement across devices.

After the malicious theft and file encryption, the data returns to the command-and-control stage, a prelude to the
extortion.

The curtain rises, revealing the chilling denouement. A
digital demand echoes through the victim's domain.

CipherSerpent reveals its fangs.

5 Troubleshooting Tactics

1. Embrace Fortification

In the digital battleground, fortifications against the looming threat of data theft are the first line of defense.

Always make an *offline* backup of your information and keep it safe.

Encrypt company critical data yourself, rendering it indecipherable to malicious eyes.

Find a company that can:

- Perform robust penetration testing to ensure your defenses are of the highest possible caliber.

- Cultivate robust cyber hygiene practices with regular audits, patches, and updates.

- Implement robust data loss prevention and back-up measures. Safeguard sensitive information, making it an impervious vault against extortion.

2. Monitor and Detect Ransomware

In the realm of digital shadows, network guardianship is key. Implement advanced monitoring and detection protocols to unveil the presence of ransomware intruders.

3. Join CiSP

Forge alliances by joining the Cyber Security Information Sharing Partnership (CiSP), where information becomes a collective shield, fortifying against future attacks.

4. Respond and Recover

Rebuild with a blueprint for resilient recovery plans to restore shattered systems to ensure a swift resurgence from the ashes of the aftermath.

5. Device Rehabilitation

Guide victims through the labyrinth of device recovery.

To Pay or Not to Pay?

That is the question for those trapped in the web of compromised accounts. What are your options? You could:

1 Enlist a Ransomware Negotiation Service

Diplomats in extortion, these specialized brokers navigate the treacherous path on your behalf to reduce the toll. Of course, if you pay up, there's no guarantee it won't happen again. On the other hand, if you don't, there may be consequences.

2. Fortify your defenses

Incorporate the lessons learned and fortify against the resurgence of hostility. Future-proof your defenses.

3. Foster education and awareness

Knowledge empowers individuals and organizations to navigate the ever-shifting tides of cyber threats.

Deceptive Charades

How Vishing Preys on Human Vulnerabilities

Nina Lopez was charmed when she answered a call from the retail outlet she worked at, and the caller slipped smoothly into her mother tongue.

"Good afternoon, am I speaking with Nina Lopez?

Nina: Yes. How can I help you today?

"*Gracias, Nina. Soy Martín Bloch, de la central.*" He continued in perfect Spanish, saying he needed her help fixing an internal system error before customer problems set in.

They had the critical updated solutions in a file on their OneDrive. He would send her the direct link to the file.

They needed her to download it and follow the instructions. Right away, please. *La eficiencia es clave aquí, Nina.*"

Nina hastened to obey, intimidated and flattered she'd been singled out for such an important mission. She'd check her email at once. Driven by her commitment to the company, Nina stepped into the scammer's web spun from silken threads of urgency.

How the Scam Works

Vishing manipulates individuals over the phone to execute potentially harmful actions, focusing on human vulnerabilities rather than technical weaknesses.

The adversary, with fluency in the victim's native language and a spoofed headquarters number, targeted the retail outlet's employee and persuaded her to access a compromised OneDrive, housing a malicious zip file.

By following instructions and downloading, extracting, and executing the zip file's contents, she unknowingly initiated a sequence that led to a major problem for the company.

The zip file concealed a file named CITFIX#29-ERD.lnk, a shortcut file, and a folder labeled 'extra.'

The .lnk file invoked a legitimate Microsoft tool called ADExplorer, concealed within the extra folder when clicked.

Simultaneously, a separate .dll file employed a technique known as 'dll sideloading,' exploiting the way Windows loads .dlls into processes.

The malicious software copied itself onto the hard drive and established a scheduled task, hijacking ADExplorer. exe, a legitimate tool to enable the extraction.

- More Reading: Vishing: What you need to know to stay safe in 2024[1]

3 Ways to Slip the Vishing Net

Mitigation and prevention are your best safeguards against vishing attacks.

User Awareness to Spot Red Flags:

- Educate employees on voice phishing techniques through internal discussions.

- Emphasize the importance of recognizing vishing calls and their potential consequences.

Implement a Policy

- Incorporate authentication measures for receiving calls from the IT department.

- Utilize internal verification methods, such as store or staff numbers, to validate the authenticity of incoming calls.

A Managed Security Service Provider

Employ a well-configured Endpoint Detection and Response EDR solution that includes:

- Real-Time Monitoring: Continuous checks for suspicious behavior or anomalies in real-time.

- Threat Detection: Using behavioral analysis and machine learning to identify potential security threats.

- Incident Investigation: Providing tools for security analysts to investigate incidents, analyze historical data, and track the progression of an attack.

- Response Capabilities: Swiftly isolating compromised devices, removing malicious files, and taking other necessary actions to contain a threat.

- Forensic Analysis: Features for detailed forensic analysis help organizations understand the scope and impact of security incidents.

- Integration with SIEM: EDR solutions may integrate with Security Information and Event Management (SIEM)

- Threat Intelligence and IoC Lists for Proactive Defense

Texts and SOS Traps

Decoding Smishing or SMS Phishing

As Jane eagerly anticipated the arrival of a long-awaited package, a buzzing sound from her phone interrupted her reverie. A text message claiming to be a delivery notification had arrived, presenting itself as a lifeline to real-time updates on her package's journey.

The seemingly innocent tracking link beckoned, and without a second thought, Jane clicked, unknowingly stepping into the treacherous realm of a smishing attack.

Unraveling the Impact

The repercussions of Jane's unwitting participation in the smishing scheme quickly unfolded. Her personal information, once guarded, became a tool for cybercriminals. Unauthorized access to her sensitive data opened the door to potential identity theft, financial exploitation, and the looming threat of fraudulent activities.

As Jane's trust in seemingly harmless SMS notifications was shattered, the invasive nature of smishing revealed the insidious tactics employed by cybercriminals. The consequences of her click extended beyond a momentary lapse in judgment; they left her vulnerable to the malicious intentions of unseen adversaries.

Spot the difference?

citibank.com is not the same as citibank.com
(The first version is correct. The second is from hackers.)
The 'a' in the second URL is a cyrillic alphabet
'a' – almost impossible for the average person to spot.

3 Ways Smishing Works

1 Crafting the Illusion

Cybercriminals adeptly pose as trusted entities, deploying urgent or enticing content to lure unsuspecting users into immediate action.

2 Deceptive Links

The fraudulent messages lead victims to malicious websites, cunningly disguised with URL shorteners or spoofed domains, where personal information becomes the unwitting sacrifice.

3 Exploiting Trust

Scammers exploit common expectations, such as awaiting delivery, and manipulate victims with a false sense of urgency that becomes the key to their trap.

7 Ways to Fend off Smishing Attacks

1. Verify Before You Click
   Scrutinize the sender's identity and refrain from clicking on links without confirmation through official channels.

2. Financial Alerts Sans Links
   Recognize that legitimate financial institutions never embed clickable links in text messages; treat such messages as potential red flags.

3. Skepticism on Raffle Wins
   Approach unexpected text messages about contest wins cautiously, verifying details through official channels.

4. Two-Factor Authentication Awareness
   Enhance security by avoiding sharing Two-Factor Authentication (2FA) codes via text; opt for authenticator apps instead.

5. Tax Season Vigilance
   Be cautious of SMS messages regarding payments and tax refunds; verify through official channels, as tax agencies communicate securely.

6. CEO Contact Verification

Authenticate urgent requests from superiors through proper channels; cross-verify CEO-related text requests with direct superiors or official channels.

7. Ignore and Move On

When in doubt, refrain from engaging with suspicious messages; legitimate communications from authorities use official channels for critical updates.

In the rapidly evolving landscape of cyber threats, staying informed and proactive is paramount.

Understanding the intricacies of smishing and adopting protective measures empower individuals to fortify their digital defenses against the deceptive allure of SMS-based attacks.

As the digital world continues to evolve, vigilance becomes the ultimate shield in the battle against cybercrime.

CONCLUSION

An ever-evolving dance

CYBER TRICKERY IS HERE to stay, but you now have the tools to ward off scammers.

Let the delete button be your discerning guardian against the temptation of suspicious links. Discretion, too, is a potent ally. Guard your privacy, revealing only what is essential. Protect sensitive details like home addresses and phone numbers from the probing algorithms seeking vulnerabilities. Never share sensitive information like Social Security numbers or bank credentials with online acquaintances.

The digital doors swing open only for the familiar. Strangers may be conduits of potential vulnerability capable of accessing your details. Choose carefully, guard against unknown friend requests, and become a digital sleuth in the masquerade. Peel away deceptive layers and pretenders with reverse image searches. Twirl only with authenticity in the dance of online connections,

Restrict the flow of information, for in the dance of deception, what remains hidden remains invulnerable and empowers your defense.

Enable Two-Factor Authentication and bolster the foundations of your digital existence. Regularly update your software to prevent hackers from infiltrating through outdated systems. Fortify the foundations and navigate securely in the digital ocean.

Let these guidelines be your enduring wisdom to master your digital realm.

Glossary of Terms

Individual and Corporate Scams

Advanced Persistent Threat (APT): A prolonged and targeted cyber-attack where an unauthorized user gains access to a network and remains undetected for an extended period.

Botnet: A network of compromised computers controlled by a single entity for malicious purposes, such as launching coordinated attacks.

Brute Force Attack: Systematically trying all possible combinations of passwords until the correct one is found, gaining unauthorized access to an account.

Credential Stuffing: An attack where cybercriminals use previously leaked username and password combinations to gain unauthorized access to multiple accounts.

Cross-Site Request Forgery (CSRF): A malicious website tricks a user's browser into performing actions on another website without their knowledge or consent.

Cross-Site Scripting (XSS): Malicious scripts are injected into web pages, allowing attackers to steal sensitive information from users.

Cryptojacking is the unauthorized use of a person's computer to mine cryptocurrency, often achieved through malware or malicious scripts.

Deep Fake: The use of artificial intelligence to create realistic-looking fake content, often in manipulated videos or audio recordings.

Denial of Service (DoS) Attack: A DoS Attack overwhelms a system, network, or website with excessive traffic, causing a disruption or making it unavailable to legitimate users.

DNS Spoofing is a way of manipulating the Domain Name System (DNS) to redirect users to malicious websites, which can lead to potential data theft or manipulation.

Eavesdropping is the unauthorized interception of electronic communications to obtain sensitive information without the knowledge or consent of the parties involved.

Keylogger: A type of malware that records keystrokes on a device, enabling cybercriminals to capture sensitive information like passwords and credit card details.

Logic Bomb: Code inserted into a software system that triggers a malicious function when specific conditions are met, often causing system disruption.

Malware: Malware is short for malicious software, and it's designed to harm or exploit devices, networks, or users.

Man-in-the-middle (MitM) Attack: An unauthorized third party intercepts and possibly alters the communication between two parties without their knowledge.

Pig Butchering: The deceptive tactics employed in online investment schemes, where scammers manipulate individuals into believing false promises, resulting in financial losses. Usage: Individual

Phishing is a fraudulent attempt to obtain sensitive information, such as usernames, passwords, and credit card details, by disguising it as a trustworthy entity in electronic communication.

Piracy: The unauthorized reproduction or distribution of copyrighted material, often facilitated through illegal online channels.

Ransomware is malicious software that encrypts a user's files and demands payment in exchange for restoring access to them. It is used mostly by Corporations but also by Individuals.

SMS-based Attacks or Smishing: Text messages deceive individuals into providing sensitive information or clicking on malicious links.

Social Engineering is a psychological manipulation technique cybercriminals use to exploit human behavior and trick individuals into divulging confidential information.

Spear Phishing: A targeted form of phishing where cybercriminals tailor their deceptive messages to a specific individual or organization using personalized information. Usage: Corporate

Spoofing involves manipulating data to appear as if it originates from a trustworthy source. Cybercriminals use this technique to deceive recipients and gain unauthorized access to sensitive information.

Texts and SMS SOS Traps: Text messages deceive individuals into providing sensitive information or clicking on malicious links.

Trojan Horse: A type of malware disguised as legitimate software, tricking users into installing it and allowing unauthorized access to their system.

Vishing: Scammers use voice communication to deceive individuals into revealing sensitive information.

Whale Fishing: Targeting high-profile individuals or executives within an organization for cyber-attacks to gain access to valuable corporate information. Usage: Corporate

Zero-Day Exploit: Definition: A Zero-Day Exploit targets software vulnerabilities unknown to the vendor, exploiting them before a fix or patch is available.

Were the 9 tales useful to you?

If so, please rate or leave a quick review

That way, others can benefit, too. Thank you!

HERE'S THE LINK, OR scan the QR code.

www.ingramcontent.com/pod-product-compliance
Lightning Source LLC
Chambersburg PA
CBHW060950050326
40689CB00012B/2622